AF593624

my notebook

ERIC CANTONA

my notebook

WEIDENFELD & NICOLSON

Flip: Good morning to you, Mr Flop. And to me too, good morning.
Flop: I'm with you, I understand.
Flip: Do you see me now?
Flop: You're a bit blurry, but yes, alive.
Flip: If I have a rendezvous then I forgot myself.
Flop: By all means please, go ahead and 'answer'.
Flip: What's the point? I'm not here.
Flop: Do you bore?
Flip: Others perhaps.
Flop: Others?
Flip: That's the space they give you. Others are us.
Flop: That might be the case, but it's as if we're invisible.
Flip: The virtual is on every street corner.
Flop: On the terrace of cafés.
Flip: What we offer to boredom is the humble creation of the moment.
Flop: Nothingness.
Flip: Nothingness is disposable, erasable, but always the source of inspiration.
Flop: So what do you do?
Flip: I fill notebooks.
Flop: Like a glass that you'd fill on this terrace.
Flip: Like a glass half empty.
Flop: And full of questions.

Flip: Abstract answers to nothingness.

Flop: To the questions that nourish you.

Flip: What nourishes me are neither the questions nor the answers.

Flop: To each answer there are questions.

Flip: Not necessarily the ones we ask ourselves. I enjoy answering aside.

Flop: That's exactly the question I was asking myself.

Flip: You see!

Flop: It's a bit blurry.

Flip: Giving an answer is pretentious, truth is blurry. I'd even go as far as to say boring.

Flop: In theory, yes.

Flip: Ah! In practice!

Flop: What are these sketches?

Flip: These sketches are you, me, they're a missed rendezvous, blurry, but true . . . A semblance of truth. For a fleeting moment, perhaps.

Flop: A rendezvous with yourself, I see.

Flip: With he who is still a stranger to me.

Flop: I understand better.

Flip: There is so much to take from everyone.

Flop: I'm understanding better and better.

Flip: I'm beginning to worry about you.

Flop: But if it worries you, then . . .

Flip: Stop! Look around instead. And travel if you have the energy or the will.

Flop: I understand.

Flip: Yes, so do I. You're taking the shape of a notebook.

Flop: Excuse me, I will leave you to your sketches and captions.

Flip: Reflections I would humbly call them.
Farewell to myself. And love me always.

Flop: Always.

horizon
vertical

vertical
horizon

Le paradis
a des rondeurs

heaven is
shapely

saisir
sa
chance

seize
your
chance

comme
une image

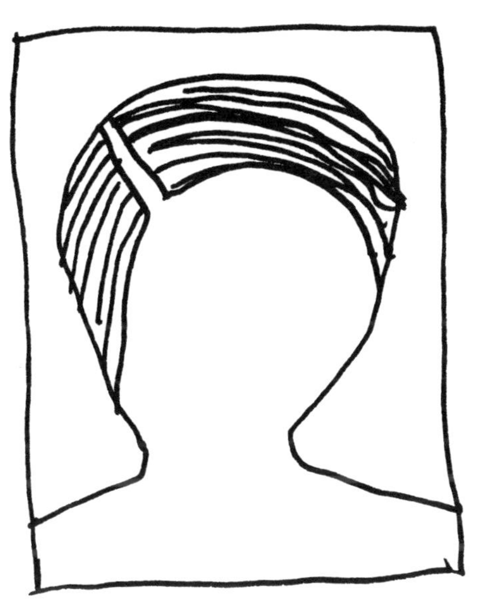

like
an image

la vie après la mort

life
after
death

incertitude?

uncertainty?

un point
c'est tout

and that's
that

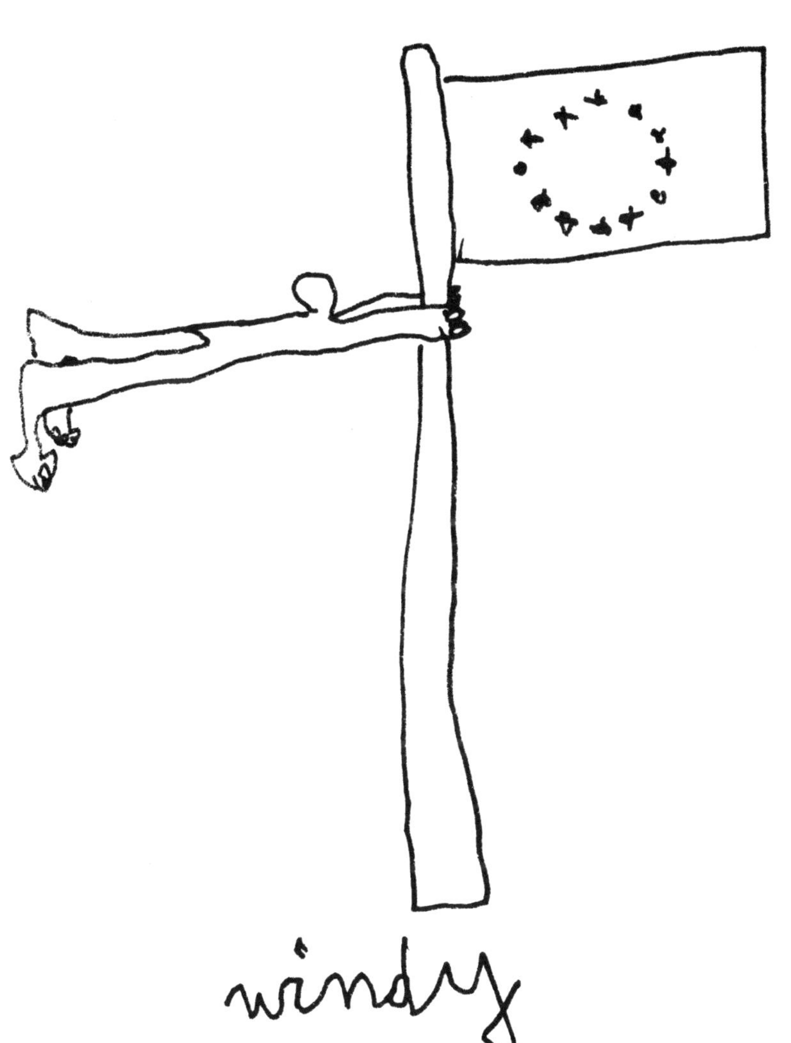
windy

face à soi-même

me

and

myself

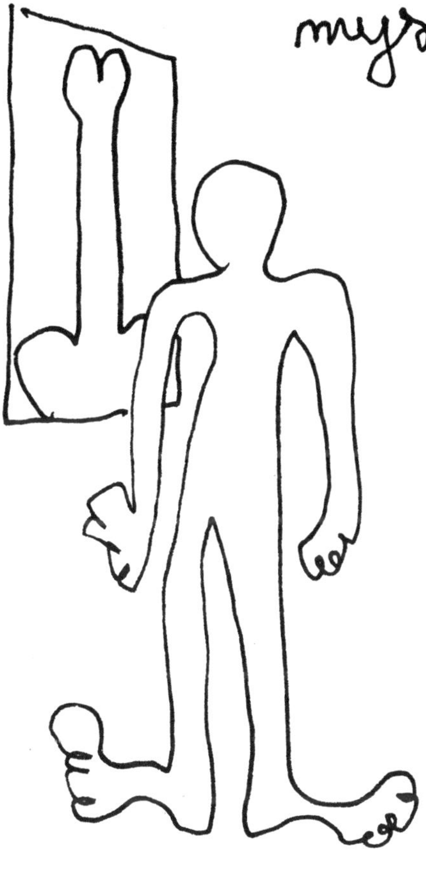

les pieds dans le plat

putting
your foot
in it

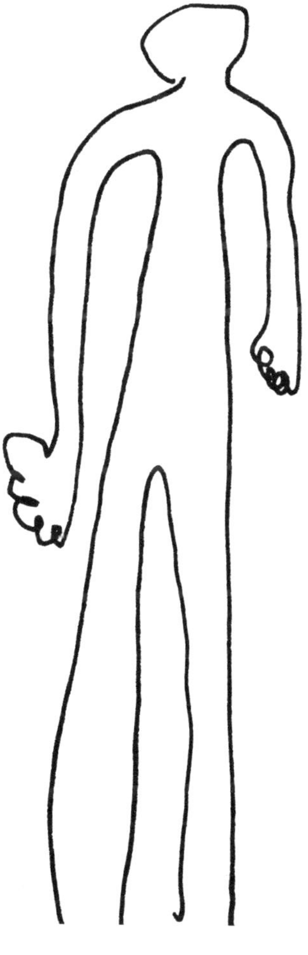

ils ont
perdu la
tête

they've lost
their
minds

l'envers

du décor

seen
from the
other side

bateau ivre
à marée basse

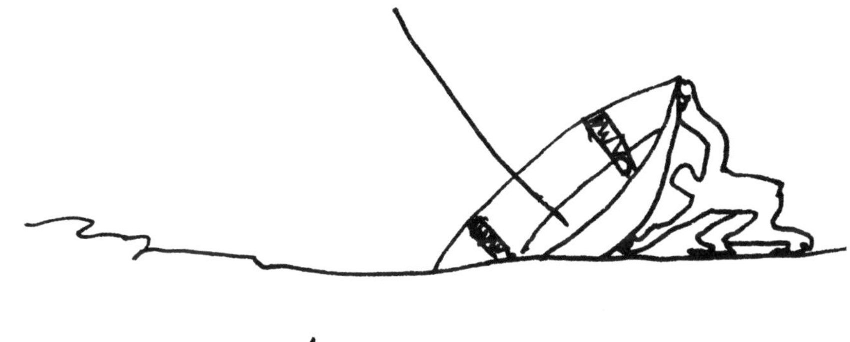

drunken ship
at low tide

désespoir

despair

je croyais
que les étoiles
c'étaient des
fenêtres

i thought
the stars
were
windows

révolte
des
petits

the little
people's
rebellion

Il aurait
oublié ses
skis

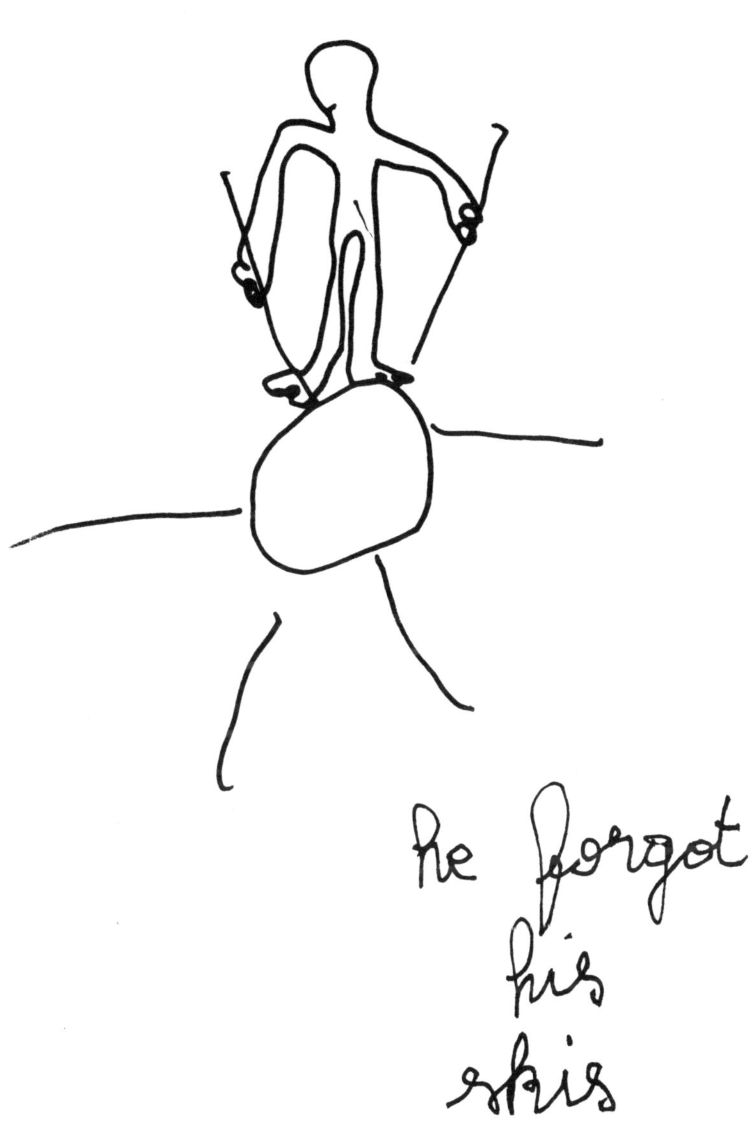
he forgot
his
skis

la mort
à
l'échelle
de la
vie

death
on the
scale
of life

éternel

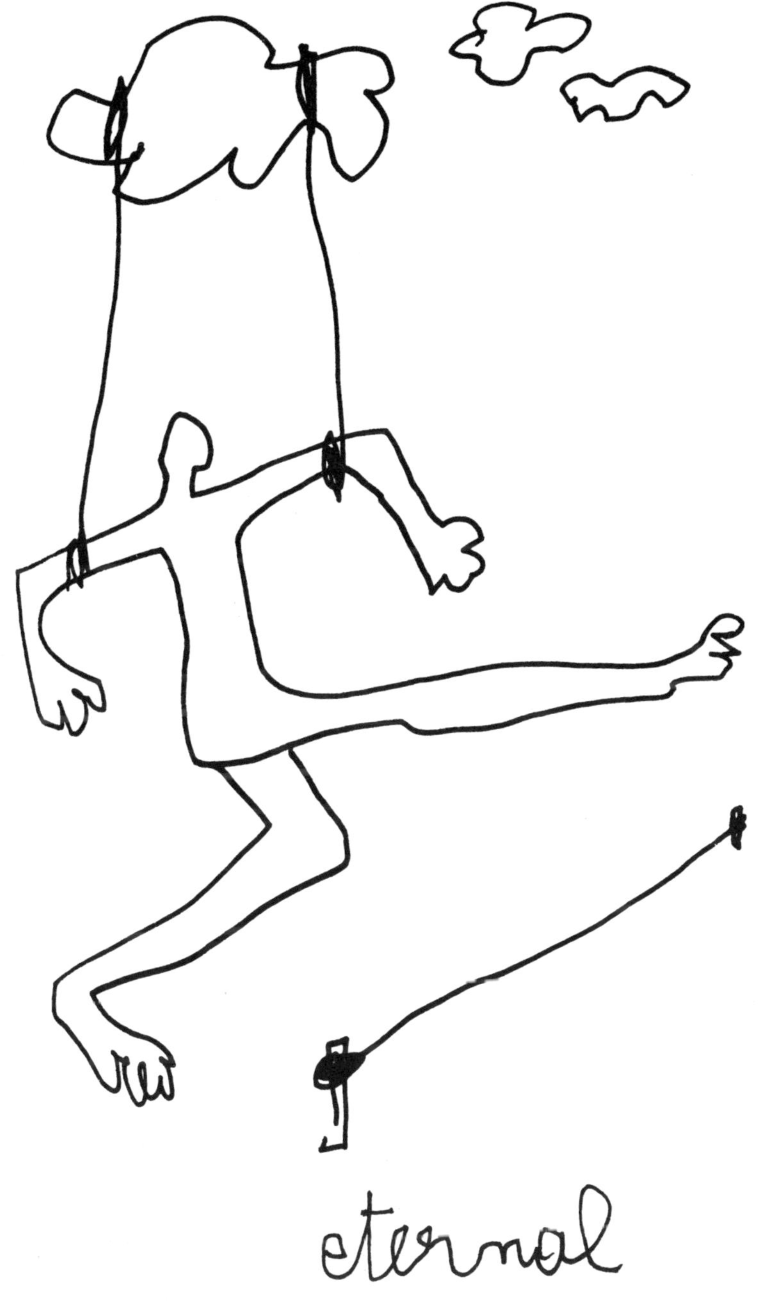
eternal

courage!

courage!

si tout n'est
pas carré
je tourne en
rond

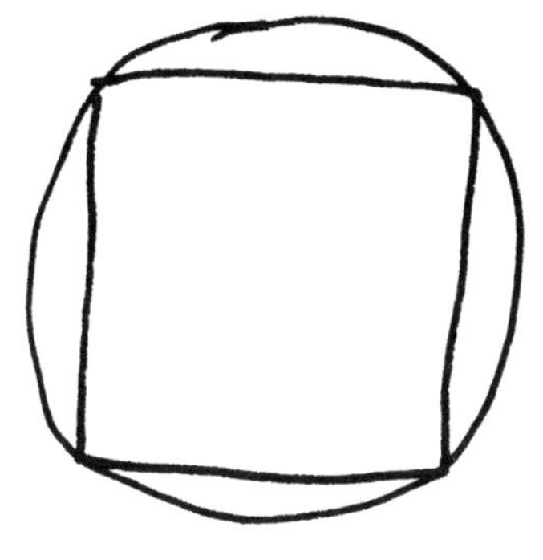

if everything
isn't squared
i go in
circles

de cause
à
effet

from cause
to
effect

les petits poissons dans l'eau

the little fish in the water

? + ! = †

? + † = !

! + † = ?

?

regardez
bien cet
homme

Look closely
at this
man

frontières

borders

the plane
is full

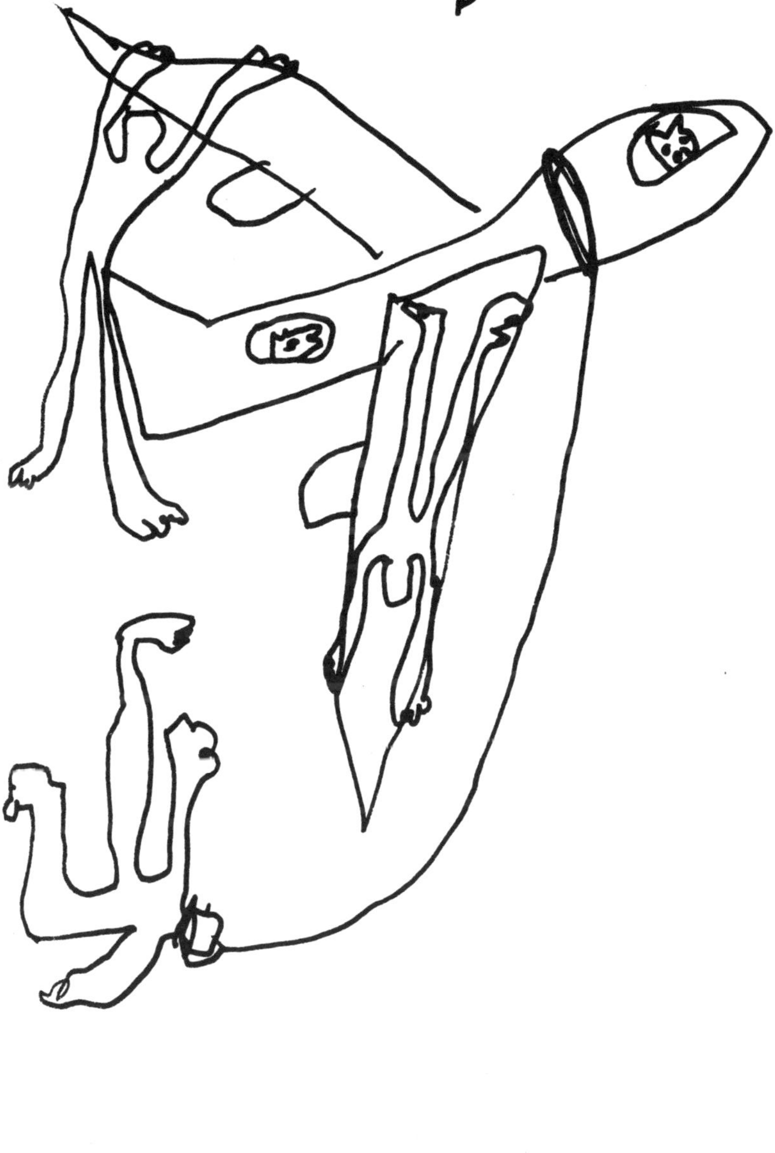

rien
à cacher
juste le
cul qui
gratte

nothing
to hide
just an
itchy
arse

temps
orageux

stormy
weather

oh my ghost!

les peaux
mortes
des géants
et le
sous marin
du pauvre

the giants' dead
skin
and the
poor man's
submarine

revanche

revenge

l'égo
en promenade

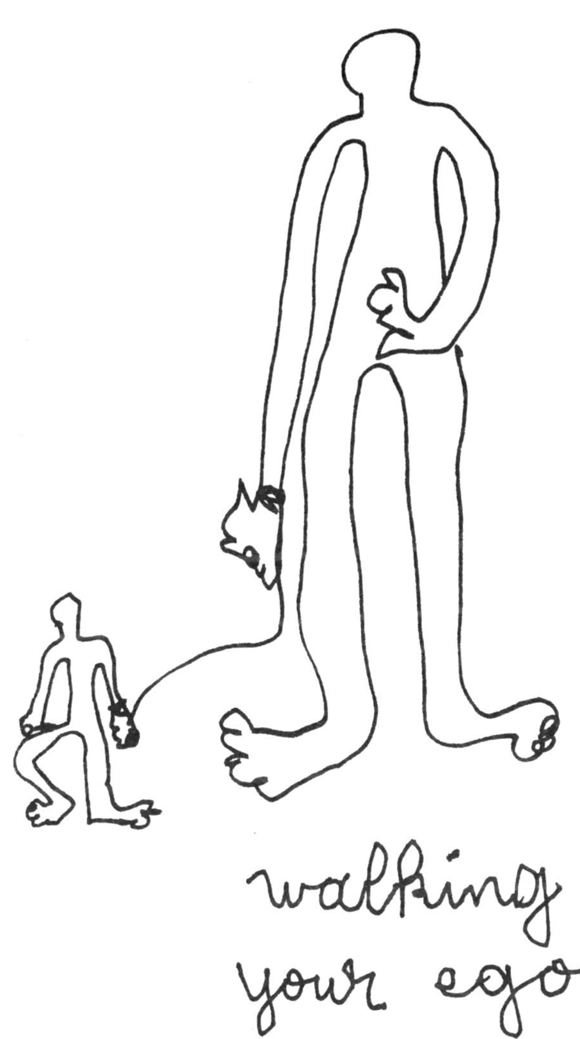
walking
your ego

cœur
de cible

heart
of the target

à l'horizon
tout va bien

all well behind
the horizon

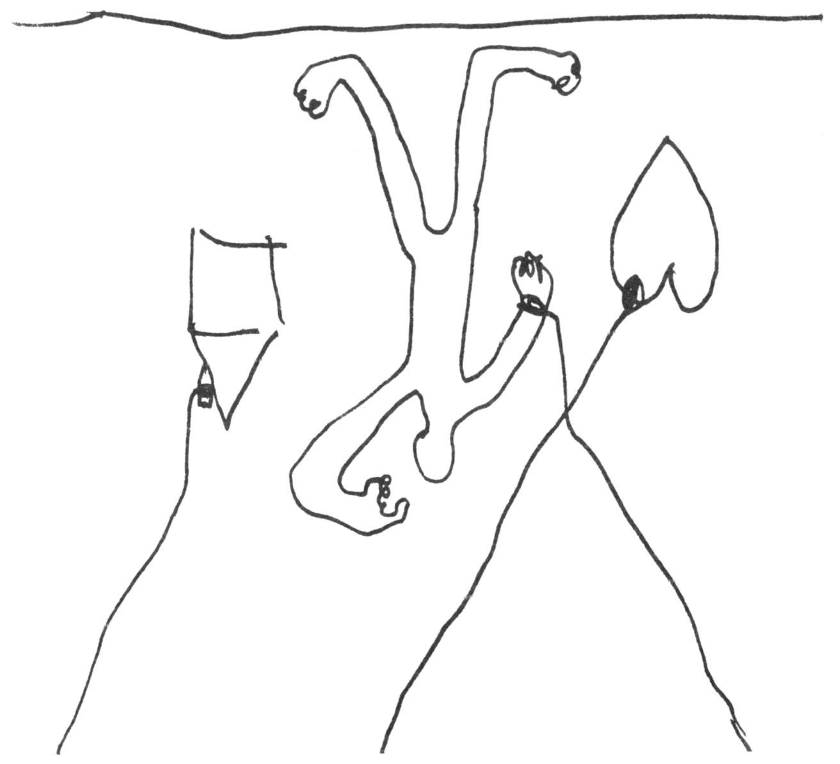

assayez

vous!

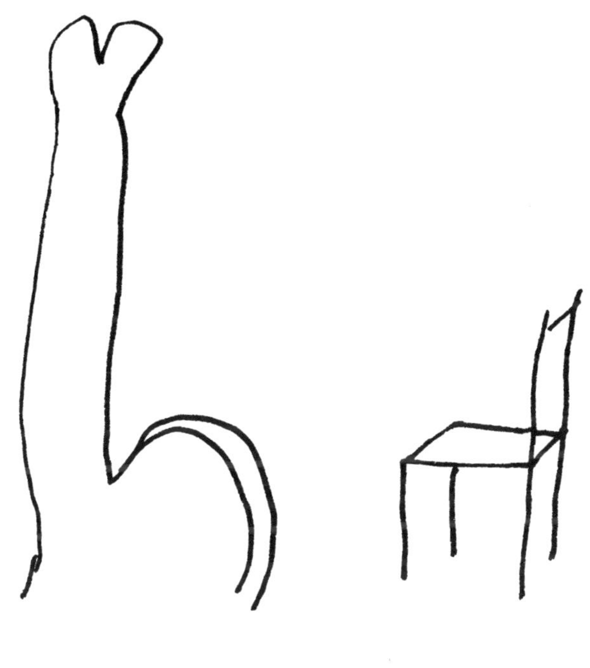

have a
seat

solidaires

solidarity

le voyage
du virtuel
et
l'homme
invisible

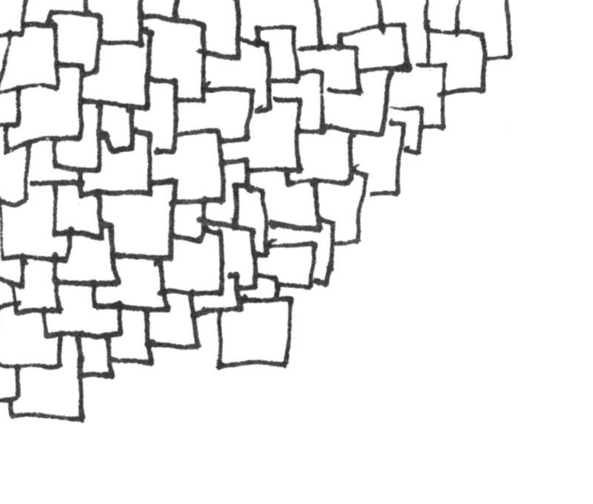

the virtual journey and the invisible man

sommeil

sleep

le cri

the scream

la crise

the crisis

les coeurs
aiment
les bras
longs

hearts
love
long
arms

RÉVOLVER

REVOLVER

l'homme
qui préférait
les arbres

the man
who preferred
trees

celle
qui préférait
les arbres
aux
Cha ignons

CABARET

the woman
who preferred
trees
to
mushrooms

CABARET

pour un
verre à moitié
vide

for a glass half-empty

péter
plus
haut que
son
cul

farts
higher
than
his
arse

à l'ombre
de 
la
main
de
dieu

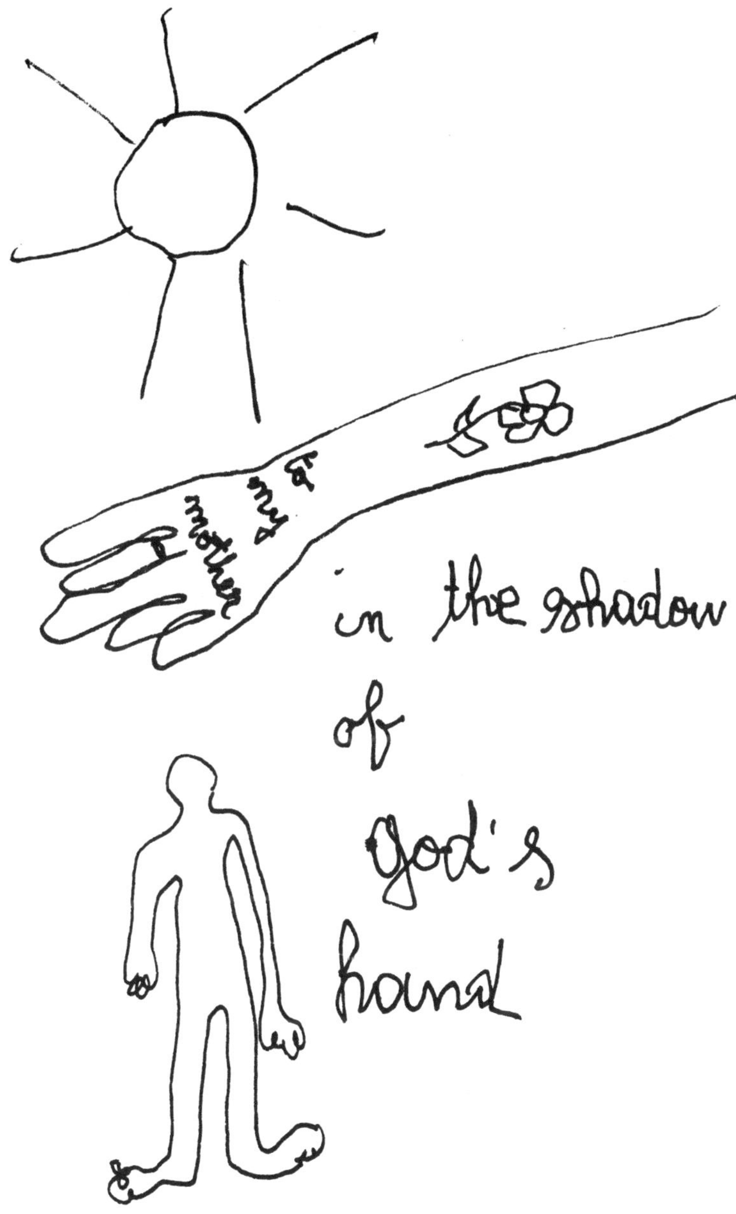

to my mother
in the shadow of God's hand

réparation

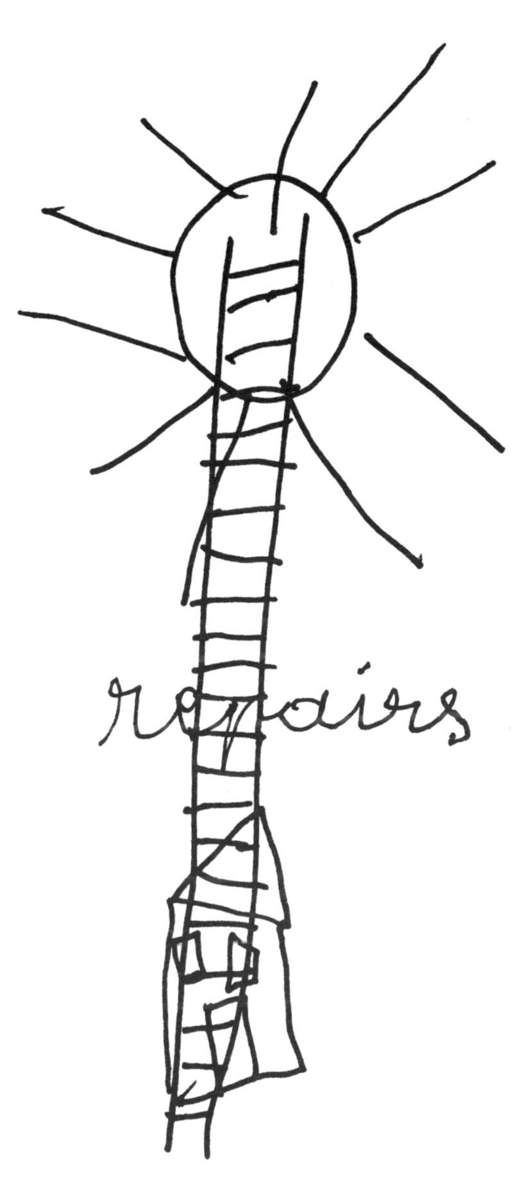
repairs

give me
a fork

que le
son

only
sound

le corps
mort du ver
est mangé
par les hommes

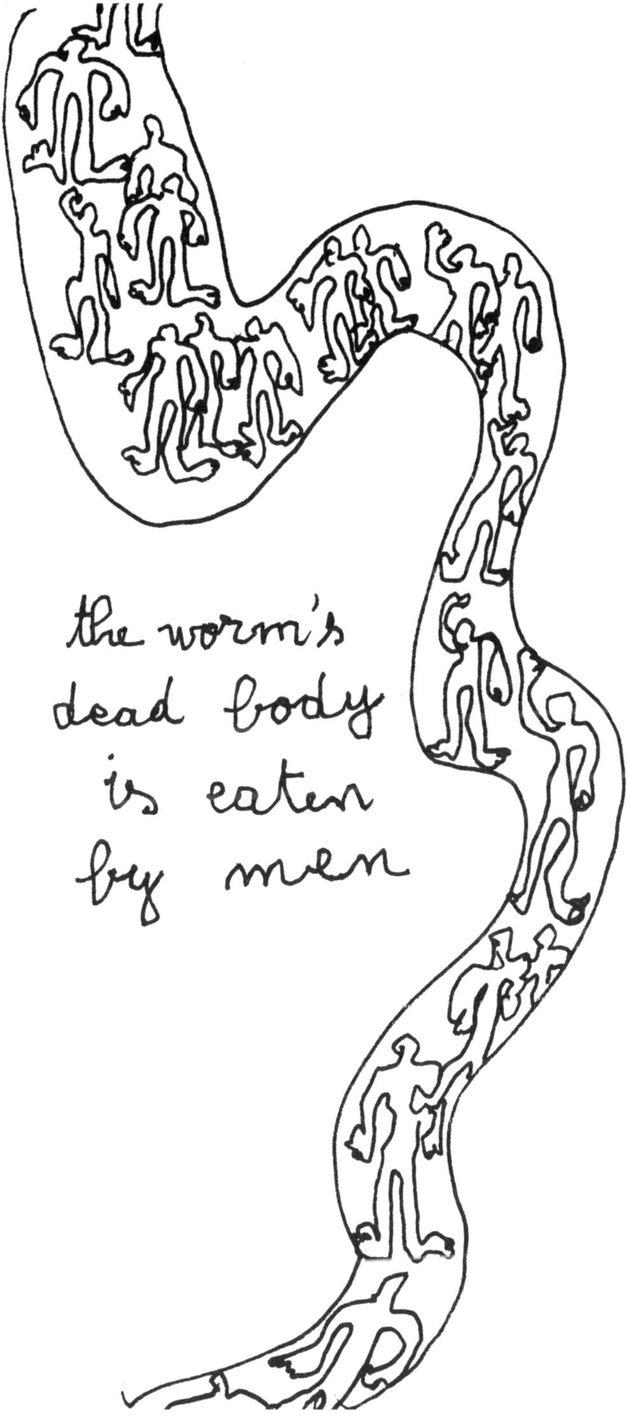

the worm's
dead body
is eaten
by men

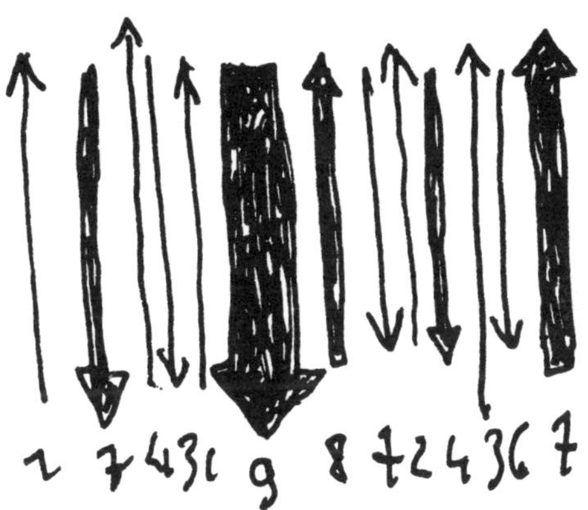

UP
AND
DOWN
END
UP

quartier
résidentiel

residential
neighbourhood

quand
je serai
grand
je serai
menteur

when i
grow up
i will
be a
liar

retour de
pleine lune

return of

the full moon

si j'étais
toi
je serais gris

if i were
you
i'd be grey

l'homme
a trouvé
le chemin
du paradis

the man
who found
the stairway
to heaven

Retour du paradis

Return
to heaven

sortie
interdite

no exit

à la table des géants

at the
giant's
table

dans
la lune

in

the moon

plus
rapide
que
son
ombre

faster
than
his
shadow

un
escalier
à
épouser

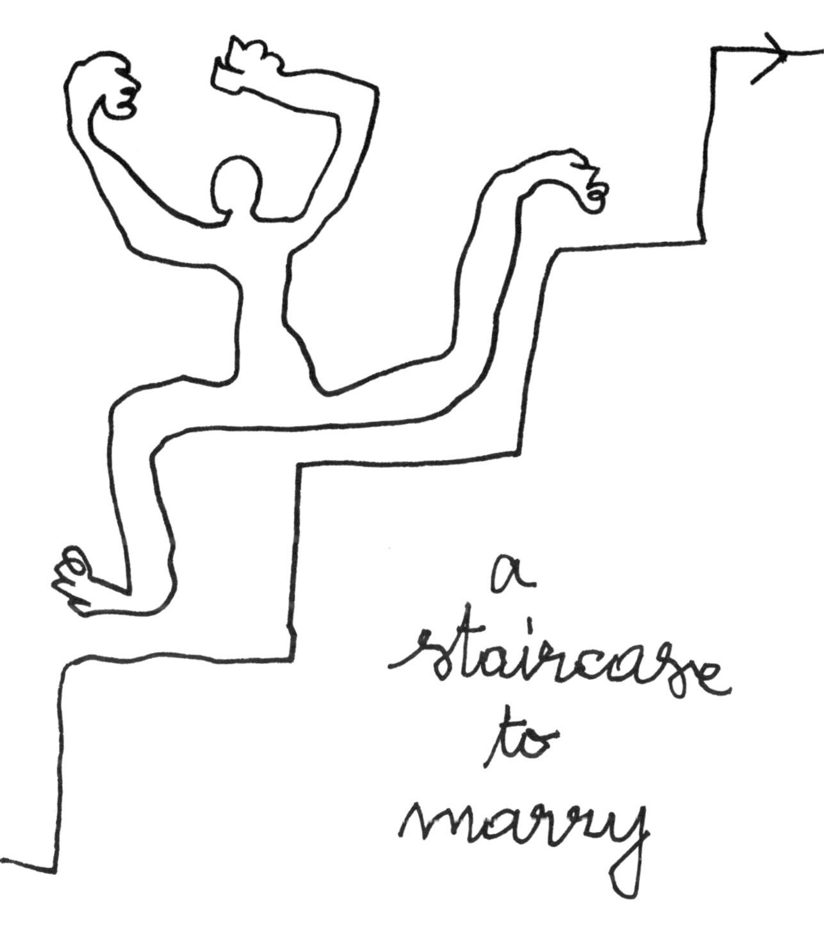
a
staircase
to
marry

de
peur
qu'elle
ne tombe

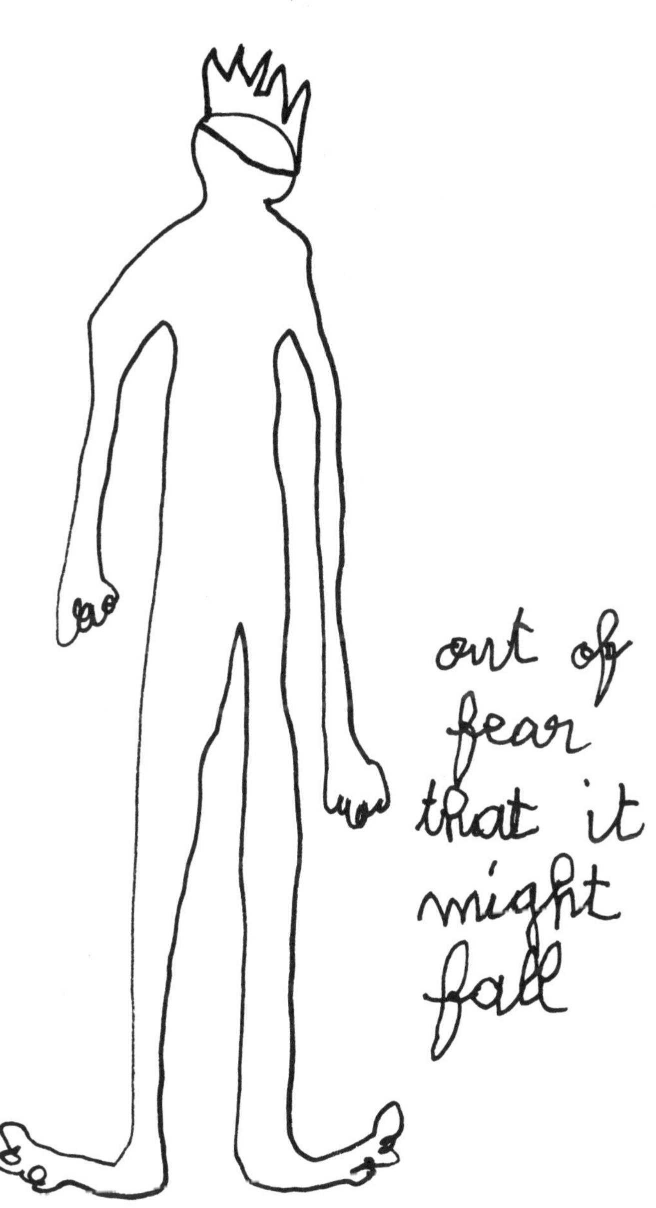
out of
fear
that it
might
fall

expression
de la
tragédie

expression
of
tragedy

la source
du village

the source
of the village

rêverie

toi

you

neige

noire

black
snow

comme
un
pied

two
left
feet

Libre

free

grandir

encore

still

growing

jalousie

jealousy

sans abri

shelterless

dieu
est
vivant

god
is
alive

don
de soi

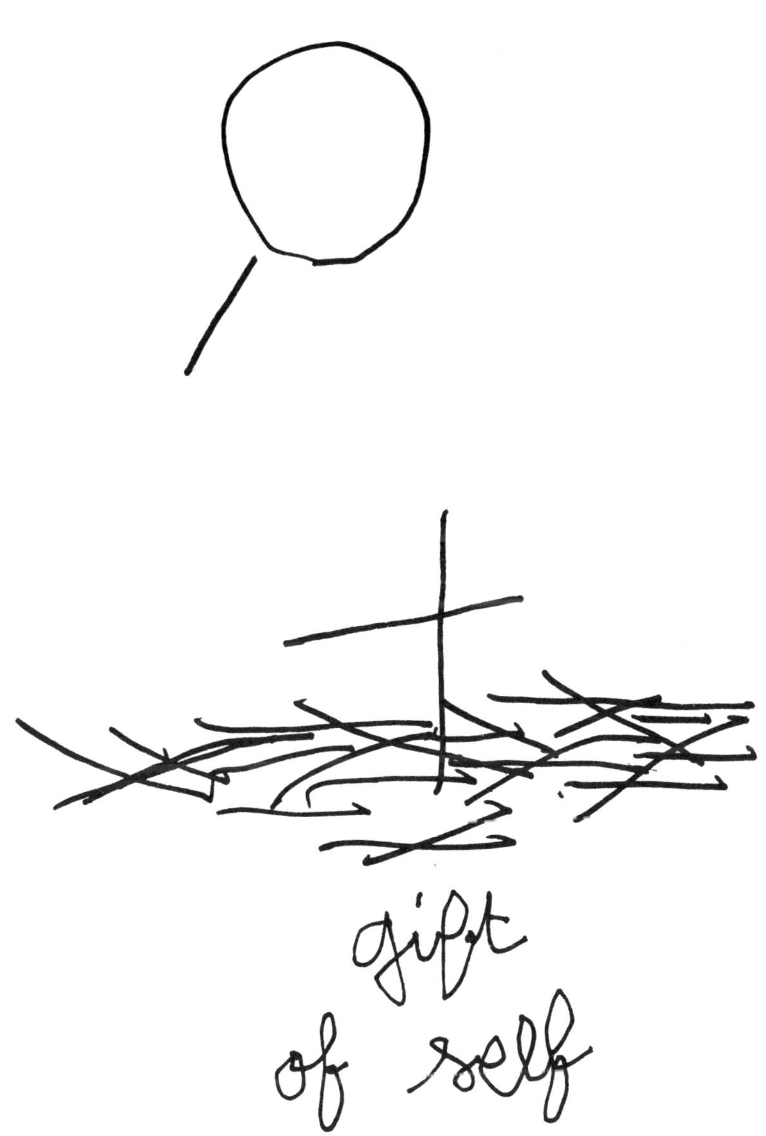
gift
of self

ceci
n'est pas
une
bite

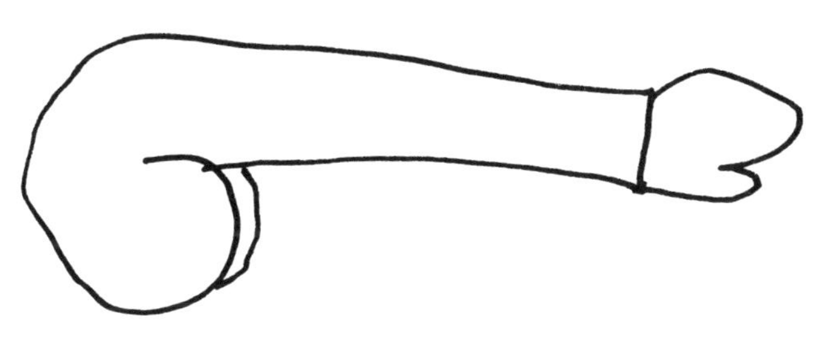

this
is not
a
cock

ceci
est une
bite

this
is a
cock

la route
est longue

the road
is long

AMOUR

planter
les clous
à la mode de chez
nous

LOVE
nailing
it
our
way

traffic light

X

intégration

integration

Mauvais Conseil

bad

advice

sans

fin

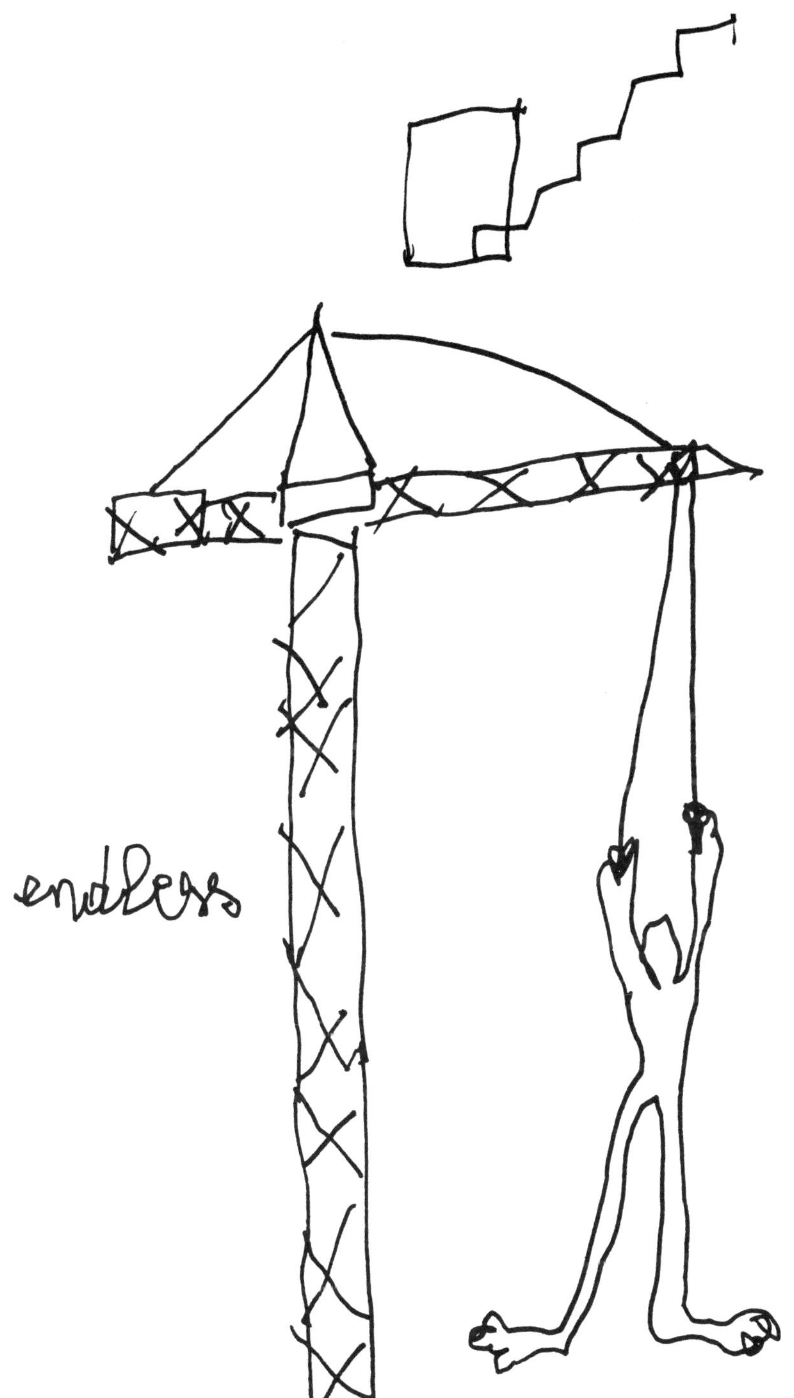
endless

lorsqu'il
sera question
de donner
des réponses

when it will
be about
time to give
answers

fuir mais
sans les
fleurs
artificielles

escape
but without
artificial
flowers

se
faire
enfiler

la croisée
des 2 mondes

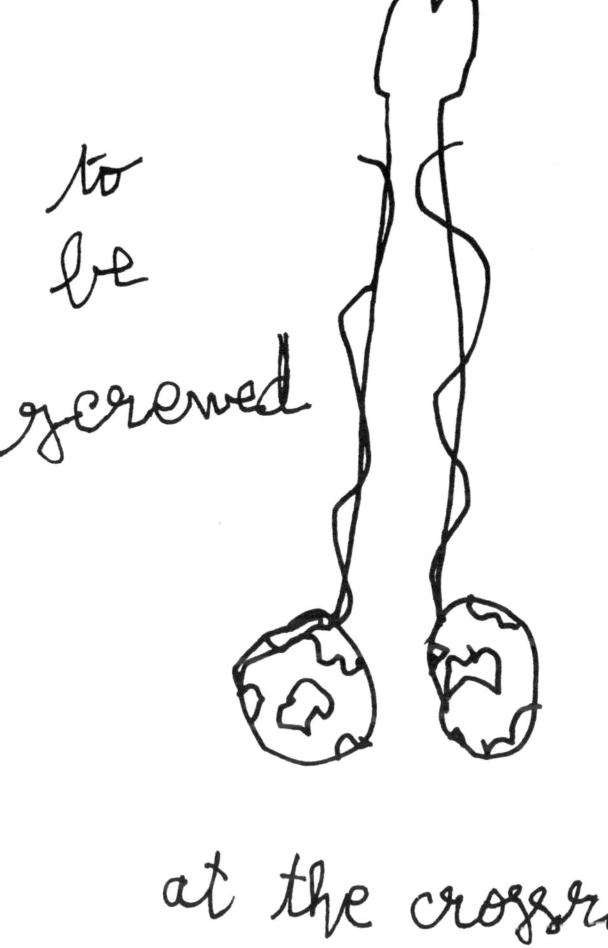

at the crossroad
of 2 worlds

orpheline

orphan
girl

tri
sélectif ?

sorting?

destin

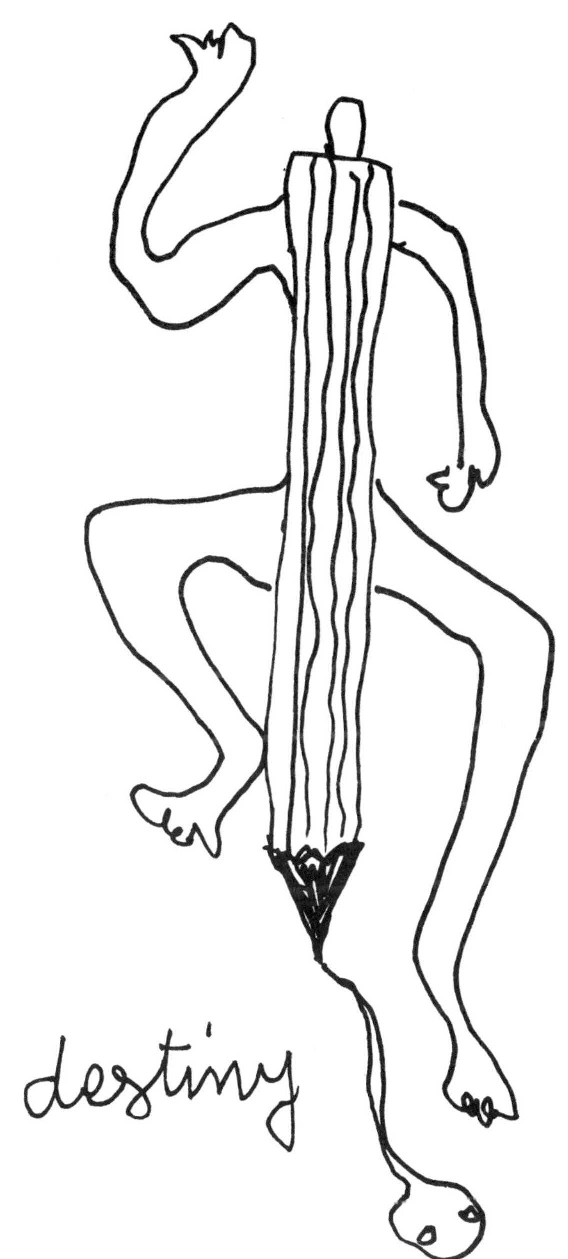
destiny

évolution

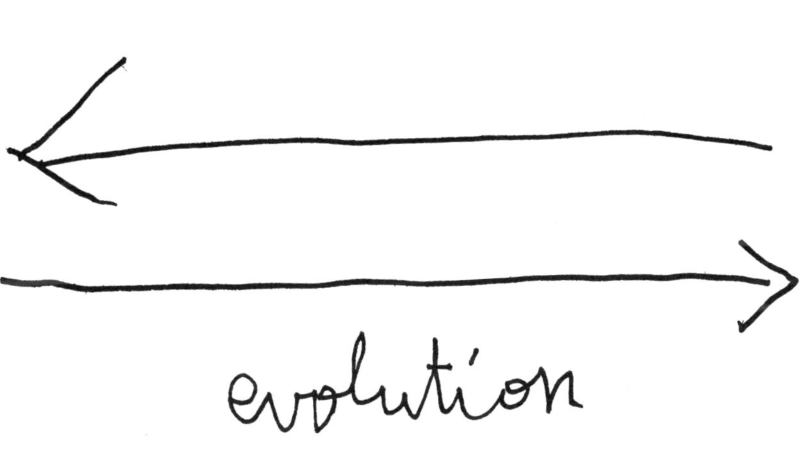
evolution

utopiste

utopian

trompe
l'oeil

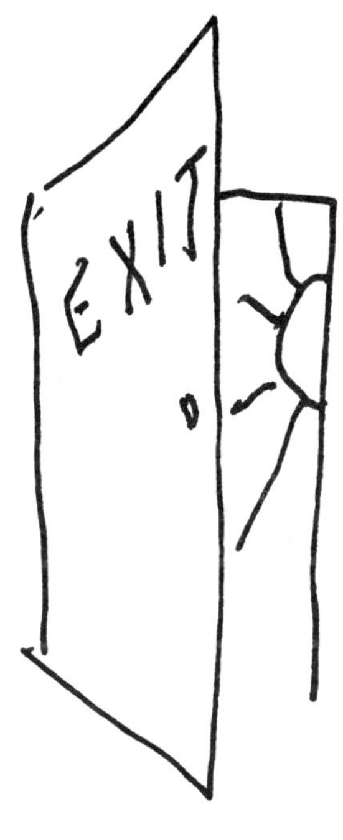

trompe
l'oeil

First published in Great Britain in 2017
by Weidenfeld & Nicolson

1 3 5 7 9 10 8 6 4 2

First published in France in 2017 as *Mon Carnet* by Flammarion

Text and illustrations by Eric Cantona
© Editions Flammarion 2017
Translation © Susanna Lea Associates 2017

All rights reserved. No part of this publication may be reproduced, stored in a retrieval system, or transmitted, in any form or by any means, electronic, mechanical, photocopying, recording or otherwise, without the prior permission of both the copyright owner and the above publisher.

The right of Eric Cantona to be identified as the author of this work has been asserted in accordance with the Copyright, Designs and Patents Act 1988.

A CIP catalogue record for this book
is available from the British Library.

ISBN HB 978 1 4746 0837 4

Printed and bound by CPI Group (UK) Ltd, Croydon, CR0 4YY

Weidenfeld & Nicolson
The Orion Publishing Group Ltd
Carmelite House
50 Victoria Embankment
London
EC4Y 0DZ
An Hachette UK Company
www.orionbooks.co.uk